T

AUSSIE WISDOM

Robert Treborlang is the author of ten previous works of fiction and non-fiction, and is well-known for his best-selling satirical tomes "How to Survive Australia", "How to be Normal in Australia", and "Staying Sane in Australia." He has written numerous stage and radio plays. He speaks eight languages and travels widely with his wife and one-eyed dog.

Other books by Robert Treborlang:

HOW TO SURVIVE AUSTRALIA

HOW TO BE NORMAL IN AUSTRALIA

HOW TO MAKE IT BIG IN AUSTRALIA

STAYING SANE IN AUSTRALIA

SYDNEY, DISCOVER THE CITY

SHE VOMITS LIKE A LADY

MEN, WOMEN AND OTHER NECESSITIES

HOW TO MATE IN AUSTRALIA

A HOP THROUGH AUSTRALIA'S HISTORY

THE LITTLE BOOK OF AUSSIE INSULTS

THE LITTLE
BOOK OF
AUSSIE
WISDOM

Collected by
Robert Treborlang

First published September, 1994

Pascal Press
PO Box 250
Glebe 2037
Australia

Copyright © Robert Treborlang
Cover and Design by Wing Ping Tong
Typeset by Badger Secretarial Services
Printed by Australian Print Group

National Library of Australia
Cataloguing-in Publication Data
Treborlang, Robert
The Little Book of Aussie Insults
ISBN 1 875 777 68 7
1. English language in Australia
2. English language — Slang
3. Australia — Language — Humour
I. Title

Distributed to newsagents by Gordon and Gotch Ltd.

Introduction

If a little knowledge is a dangerous thing then you have a very dangerous book in your hands!

This tome contains a collection of Aussie wisdom about the important and not so important things in life.

Surprising even themselves, Australians have a knack for cutting through the garbage and getting to the heart of the matter.

"A picture is worth exactly what some sucker will pay for it" (Robert Hughes), "When you can't laugh you're dead" (Beatrice Faust), "Beer makes you feel as you ought to feel without beer" (Henry Lawson) are just a few simple examples.

Unique in the history of the world, Australians have developed a philosophy all of their own. And they have a lot to be philosophical about.

After all in what other part of the globe could you get both understanding and a laugh from a saying such as "Death is about the only cheerful thing in the bush?"

At the same time Australians have always taken their wisdom for granted and often seem unaware of their distinctly unusual outlook on life.

The Little Book of Aussie Wisdom contains the many gems I have collected over the years from every day people, from books, from newspapers, from television and radio, and from many famous personalities.

Regard it as a small treasure chest. Open the lid and peer inside. Will it be fancy rags or rubies? Will it be Lang Hancock's "The best way to help the poor is not to become one of them" or Kamahl's "If life hands you a lemon, make lemonade!"

Dip into it and rummage at random.

The Little Book of Aussie Wisdom

ABC
Well, the first thing to do in life is to escape from your friends.

Henry Lawson, Poet-Writer

Act The Bunny
The British brought many things to Australia: the rabbit, the theatre. It's the rabbits who prospered.

John Romeril, Playwright

Age Of Content
No one is ever too old to know better.

Margaret Preston, Writer

Airheads Will Roll
Data isn't information, information isn't knowledge, and knowledge isn't wisdom.

Phillip Adams, Writer-Broadcaster

Alter Ego

There is more to life than yourself.

Ray Martin, Media Personality

Anglo-Biter

Being born Anglo-Saxon is a terrible handicap, because it means having to make a virtue of self-restraint.

David Dale, Writer-Journalist

Approximate

Friendship, if you know how to work it, is better than a cousin in Parliament.

Marcus Clarke, Writer

Arthuritis

I would rather trust the young for all their mistakes than people of 50, 60 and 70 whose minds have become fossilised.

Arthur Calwell, Opposition-Leader

As Luck Would Have It

Anyone who reckons luck doesn't have anything to do with success has never been successful.

John Singleton, Adman-Writer

As The Actress Said To Bishop
It's a slow climb to the penthouse, but it's a quick drop to the shithouse.

Stan Zemanek, Radio Presenter

Ashing Their Brains Out
Smoking is detrimental to the intelligence of Australians.

King O'Malley, Politician

Asking For It
We need our enemies to teach us what friends in kindness never shows.

Gwen Harwood, Poet

At A Pinch
An ounce of initiative is worth a ton of talent.

John Laws, Media Personality

At Any Cost
In the university of adversity the fees are highest but the lessons are remembered for ever.

Donald Cameron, Politician

At The Drop Of A Cad
Behind every successful woman there's usually a divorce.

Alma De Groen, Writer

At The Outside

Public opinion, my boy, is a rotten substitute for personal character.

Martin Boyd, Writer

Aussie Pursuits

Australians take trivial things seriously because they can't take serious things seriously.

Jonathon Gleeson, Shiatsu Therapist

Aussie Rules

Never open doors for others, never wear nylon socks and never eat pies at postponed race meetings.

Traditional Saying

Backing The Wrong Horse

If only the Australian workers transferred the thought they invest in picking winners and the passion they devote to football onto politics, we would have had the revolution years ago.

Ian Turner, Writer

Backtrack

The seven seas may divide the migrant from his home but he will never quite shake its dust from his feet.

Raymond Crawford, Historian

Backyard To The Future
All I can see is my own, and all I can't see is my son's.

John Batman, Colonist

Bad Taste Buds
Australia's politics have sadly deteriorated, but the palate has developed.

Bernard King, Chef-Entertainer

Bagging The Press
One more day of Australian newspapers and I'll have a plastic bag instead of a colon.

Germaine Greer, Writer-Academic

Bare Bones
I don't go in for nude bathing myself, but I think it's worth looking at.

Rupert Hamer, Premier

Barging In
Australia is a nation of boat people.

R.J. Gross, Writer

Be A Mate
If you can't say the good word, at least don't say the hard one.

Ben Chifley, Prime-Minister

Be Your Own Boss
It gives you a pleasant feeling of mastery if you are sitting in front of a television screen and you can turn it to another channel.

Sir Robert Menzies, Prime-Minister

Beat It
The man that holds his own is good enough.

Banjo Paterson, Poet-Writer

Behind The Scene
The Australian believes that to express oneself, except when asked or in a crisis, is pretentious.

Frank Graham Little, Writer

Behind The Wheel
The car's only an improved wheelbarrow.

John Shaw "Keats" Neilson, Lyric Poet

Best Foot In
Be seen, be different, stand up and be counted. Don't be pushed around, have the courage to achieve. And never lay down in life.

Warwick Capper, Footballer

Better The Devil
Everyone neglects opportunities, everyone makes blunders, everyone commits sins. These are the very conditions by which progress is made.

Catherine Spence, Novelist

Bewdy
Australia is like a Sleeping Princess on whom the dust of ages has settled.

D.H. Lawrence, Novelist

Beyond A Joke
When you can't laugh, you're dead.

Beatrice Faust, Writer

Beyond Good And Staysharp
Evil is the stone on which the good sharpens itself.

Dorothy Auchterlonie, Poet

Bill Of Health
There is no such thing as free health care.

Ralph Hunt, Politician

Blade Runner
We can never really know what is true recollection and what has been implanted there to seem true.

George Johnston, Writer

Blind Turn
Why do we insist on walking backwards towards our deaths with our eyes fixed stupidly on past chimeras?

Robert Dessaix, Writer-Critic

Blow Your Mine
The book that has most influenced my life is the Western Australian Mining Act.

Lang Hancock, Tycoon

Blue Chips
Of course we are not the original knockers. The English are more skilled at it and enjoy it more. The difference is that Australians really mean it. The knocking comes from the depths of their tortured feelings of inadequacy.

Keith Dunstan, Writer

Board The Pants Off Us
In Australia most things happen on verandahs.

Ethel Mills, Writer

Bog It In
Life's a bowl of pasta — enjoy it — have heaps!

Maria Venuti, Entertainer

Animals

There is only one place for any fur coat, and that is on the back of an animal.

Peter Singer, Writer

You can lead a horse to drink, but you can't make it water.

Sir Joh Bjelke-Petersen, Premier

The kangaroo hops with the leaps of his logic.

Osip Mandelstam, Writer

It's no good crying over spilt milk; all we can do is bail up another cow.

Ben Chifley, Prime Minister

Every owner thinks his horse has wings on its legs and a Rolls-Royce engine in its insides, and the trainer daren't deny it or he'll lose the horse.

Banjo Paterson Poet-Writer

The rabbit that runs away is the rabbit that gets shot.

Sir Thomas Blamey, Field Marshal

Bond Of Contention

The faith of men is as strong as the sympathy between them, and perhaps the hardest thing on earth for a woman to kill.

Henry Lawson, Poet-Writer

Booby Trap

If I had my way I'd put all Women's Liberationists behind bras.

Sir Leslie Herron, Jurist

Bored Stiff

It is as hard to maintain the rage as it is to maintain an erection.

Jim McClelland, Politician

Boss Cockies

Australia is the only country in the world where the peasantry make the laws.

Louis Esson, Playwright

Bottom Line

In life if you think you can, or you think you can't you are absolutely right.

Jeremy Cordeaux, Radio Presenter

Boundary Riders
A man of character realizes his limitations, however he
never accepts them.

Des Renford MBE, Sportsman

Brain Power
Intellect arrives without the aid of education and
culture.

Norman Lindsay, Artist-Writer

Bread Line
Bread is a large number of small holes entirely
surrounded by bread.

Lennie Lower, Writer

Bridge The Gap
Sydney is my city but Australia is not my country.

Peter Endrey-Walder, Surgeon

Buck's Party
On the use of the first dollar the whole of your future
may depend. It is often this that decides whether one is
to become a millionaire or a socialist.

K.J. "Australianus" Back, Writer

Bugger Of A Job
Men. Difficult to love. Difficult not to.

Judith Rodriguez, Poet

Bull Artists
Swearing is not an art in Australia as it is in Spain, it is a habit.

Thomas Wood, Writer

Bum To Mum
To live in Australia permanently is rather like going to a party and dancing all night with one's mother. There's something a little bit unhealthy about it.

Barry Humphries, Writer-Entertainer

Bummer
Australia is the arse-end of the world.

Paul Keating Prime Minister

Buzz Words
Words are the door-knockers of the house of the mind to call and awaken those within.

Dame Mary Gilmore, Poet

Buy Jingo
Nothing like a bit of hatred to create patriotism.

Peter Yeldham, Writer

By The Skin Of Your Teeth

Bite off more than you can chew — and chew like crazy.

Valerie Parv, Writer

Call Of Nature

The bush. Biggest dunny in the world. Thirty thousand square miles of the bastard.

Douglas Lockwood, Writer

Call To Account

People are judged on two points: What they have in their heads and what they have in their banks.

Bill Bowyang Magazine

Can Of Worms

Jail is perfectly designed to bring out the worst in both inmates and the people sent to guard them.

Tony Vinson, Academic

Catch 1822

There are two classes of person in New South Wales. Those who have been convicted and those who ought to have been.

Lachlan Macquarie, Governor

Can't Buy Me Louvre
When all is said and done, even money is not much good where there is no genuine culture.

D.H. Lawrence, Novelist

Cause A Stir
Radicalism is the opium of the middle class.

Christina Stead, Writer

Chafing At The Bits
We fritter away our lives in detail.

Errol Flynn, Actor

Chain-Smirker
Bullshit it's a free country. You've only got to start telling some home truths and then you see quick how bloody free a country can be.

Robert Wallace, Writer

Chancers And Dancers
We're a nation of punters and party-goers.

Paul Hogan, Actor

Change Of Life
We have built cities and roads over the Australian land, we have torn gold and coal out of it, we have pastured

sheep and cattle on it, we have spread fields of wheat and sugar-cane across it — and we have not altered it one iota. It has altered us.

Eleanor Dark, Writer

Checkmate
Most people in Australia have to see an ending to a relationship before they can begin one.

Leanne Richters, Desktop Publisher

Cherry Can
It doesn't matter if you've lost your virginity as long as you've still got the box it came in.

Anonymous Graffiti

Chuck A Seven
Of all God's miracles, death is the greatest.

Peter Porter, Poet

Ciao Brissie
Brisbane — the Naples of the southern hemisphere.

John Betjeman, Poet

Clean Sweep
You don't put on a replacement just to give the laundry a job.

Jack Gibson, Rugby League Coach

Close Encounters

The nearer a white Australian is to Aborigines the more likely he is to be a racist.

Frank Hardy, Writer

Cod's Wallop

Success is like a smack in the face with a wet fish.

Sir Sidney Nolan, Artist

Collared

What is one man's fate today, may be another's tomorrow. We are all in it up to the neck together, and we know it.

Frederic Manning, Writer

Come Clean

The sign of true self-respect is washing your hands before going to the toilet, not after.

Ian Stocks, Academic-Filmmaker

Coming While Going

Rowing is an extraordinarily apt sport for men in public life because you can face one way while going the other.

Gough Whitlam, Prime Minister

Arts

A picture is worth exactly what some sucker will pay for it.

Robert Hughes, Critic-Writer

Australians wrote with the greatest freedom there is — writing without fear of being read.

Frank Moorhouse, Writer

It's a pity that every writer couldn't put all his bitterness into one book and then burn it.

Henry Lawson, Writer

I do not recall a single utterance by a labor leader in Australia that could be construed to mean that literature meant anything to him.

Hartley Grattan, Historian

Australia has the perfect Opera House. The only problem is that the outside is in Sydney and the inside in Melbourne.

Maria Prerauer, Journalist

Fiction is a toned-down version of reality.

John Capsanis, Legal Practitioner

Complete Medical Cover
A surgeon does everything but knows nothing, a physician knows everything but does nothing, a psychiatrist knows nothing and does nothing, and a pathologist knows everything and does everything but a day too late.

John Hilton, Doctor

Consummate
Love: the highest friendship.

Rose Scott, Suffragette

Cornstalkers
Everyone's a mate in New South Wales.

Bill Hayden, Governor-General

Cot Cases
There are two men whom you should never go to Court against unless you are dragged there: one is he who has more money than you have, and the other is he who has no money at all.

K.J. "Australianus" Back, Writer

Cringe And Whinge
Mankind may be divided into two races, those who acquiesce and those who growl.

Sir Walter Murdoch, Essayist

Cross As Two Sticks

If Jesus wept over Jerusalem He must be heartbroken over Sydney.

Rev. Fred Nile, Politician

Crotchety Traveller

International travel broadens the mind but has singularly constricting effects on other portions of the anatomy.

Sir Robert Menzies, Prime Minister

Cut Above The Rest

A block of land, a brick veneer, and the motor-mower beside him in the wilderness — what more does an Australian man want to sustain him?

Allan Ashbolt, Writer

Cutting The Mustard

A good editor is a person who keeps things out of the paper.

J.F. Archibald, Publisher

Daily Mirror

In life there is sometimes little to choose between the reality of illusions and the illusion of reality.

Patrick White, Novelist

Darwin
A hell of a place to be off the grog.

Bob Hawke, Prime-Minister

Day Of The Locust
The worst thing about work in the house or the home is that whatever you do, it is destroyed, laid waste or eaten within 24 hours.

Lady Alexandra Hasluck

Dead Bird
If you squawk like a crow, look like a crow, you'll be shot like a crow.

Sir Joh Bjelke-Petersen, Premier

Dead Heart
Explorers in the interior of the Australian temperament bring back tales of a Great Emotional Desert.

A.G. Stephens, Writer

Death In Paradise
If a man gets a medal for killing an innocent person in an innocent harbour then the world is fucked.

Derryn Hinch, Writer TV Presenter

Demolition Derby
What this country should be producing most of are bulldozers.

Sorin Dascalu, Architect

Desperately Seeking
The truth, like God, does not exist — only the search for it.

Frank Hardy, Writer

Dig Bikkies
You wouldn't be an Aussie, you wouldn't be true blue, if Arnott's biscuits didn't mean something to you.

Donald Hutley, Writer

Dine Strine
Australia — a restaurant at the edge of a desert!

Yevgeny Yevtushenko, Poet

Dingo Lingo
I don't think Nature speaks English.

Les Murray, Poet

Dire Genes
Life's a bastard, and we're all bastards together.

David Martin AM, Author

Dirty Trick
The worse the crime, the less the punishment.

James Darling, Headmaster

Do A Flourish
Men and boughs break,
Praise life while you walk and wake.

David Campbell, Poet

Done To A Turn
Revolution never relieves misery but increases it.

Martin Boyd, Writer

Don't Hold Your Breath
You're far better off living than dying.

Ron Clarke, Sportsman

Don't Look Up
Not to fear men might be comparatively easy if one were allowed to scorn them.

Peter Steele, Writer

Australia

If you want to sail around Australia, navigation is easy. "Keep Australia on your left."

Hans Tholstrup, Energy Specialist

Australia will always stand as the greatest error in location the Lord ever made.

John Kenneth Galbraith, Economist

Australia is a huge rest home.

Germaine Greer, Writer-Academic

I would rather feel nostalgic about Australia than live there.

Paul Haefliger, Critic

Australia is too vast.

George Farwell, Writer

Australia is a dynamic society where men rise and fall in one generation.

John Douglas Pringle, Writer

Australia had a rough childhood.

Kate Jennings, Poet

Dotting The Line

Australia is a big blank map, and the whole people is constantly sitting over it like a committee, trying to work out the best way to fill it in.

Charles Bean, Historian

Double-Talk

Words have little relation to reality.

Martin Boyd, Writer

Double Your Debt

They who owe the most when they die, win.

Frank Daniberg, Barrister-Businessman

Down To Brass Tacks

If you want to know what's going on in a corporation or government department, patronise their lifts at 5pm.

John Capsanis, Legal Practitioner

Down Under

Australians must be the most morbidly self-critical people on earth.

James Cameron, Politician

Dry As A Stone God
Australians speak with their mouths closed to keep in the moisture.

Ian Stocks, Academic-Filmmaker

Dry Horrors
The last ones to go in a drought are the emus and the stock and station agents.

Tom Harvey, Farmer

Dung To Death
I should like to die quietly and fertilize this beautiful soil of Australia, which is far better than anything we try to say about it.

Katharine Prichard, Writer

Dust Off
Death is, perhaps, the only commonplace thing that we do not feel to be so.

William Sutherland, Physicist

Economy Downturn
When boarding an aeroplane try never to turn right.

David Gool, Traveliste

Eat Like A Bird
For a good life breakfast in Scotland, lunch in Australia, and dine in France.

Henry Kingsley, Writer

Electric Deer
Men will fawn where there is power.

Wiliam Forster, Writer

Enemy Territory
War is a different country.

Randolph Stow, Author

Even Blind Freddie
People in this country wouldn't recognize revolution if the saw it.

Louis Esson, Playwright

Exoztentialism
A dinkum Aussie judges a man by what he does, not by who he is.

Arthur Phillips, Writer

Eyes Like Roadmaps
The temperate man sees the same world always, the proper inebriate finds the world never presents the

same aspect twice.

David Ireland, Writer

Face Ache
A plain woman will have nothing forgiven her.

Miles Franklin, Writer

Fail Safe
Australians love a good loser.

James Killen, Politician

Fair Going Over
No man should be robbed except by the proper business methods.

Lennie Lower, Writer

Fair To Middling
To be nice is better than being stimulating, or analytical, or witty.

Mary Liverani, Writer

Fall Out
In a country without seasons or crops the passage of time is marked by receding hairlines and the cooling affections of those we love.

Ian Beck, Writer

Fault-Lines

Nobody ever goes broke without making a mistake.

Sir Paul Strasser, Businessman

Feeling Chipper

Australians on the whole are a well-balanced people. They have a chip on both shoulders.

Mark Berriman, Vegetarian Activist

Feeling Down

There is nothing but the human touch can heal the human woe.

Victor Daley, Poet

Fete Worse Than Death

The great festivals of Australia have to do not with religion or politics but with outdoor physical struggle.

Ross Terrill, Writer

Fighting Mad

Man is a challenge seeking animal and if he's alone on a desert island he'll invent a game with three stones that he might lose.

Bob Ellis, Writer-Filmmaker

Canberra

The difficulty with Canberra is to find it.
Malcolm Muggeridge, Writer

The world's first do-it-yourself capital.
Robin Boyd, Writer

Canberra is like a woman expensively coiffured, dressed, and made-up, well-educated, courteous — and frigid.
Don Dunstan, Premier

Canberra has been constructed as though it were in the tropics.
Ernest Crutchley, Diplomat

Canberra. A beautifully landscaped retirement village.
Rolf Jensen, Academic

The only good view of the place was out of the back window of a car speeding north.
Mungo MacCallum, Writer

Filigreed

In Australia it is considered more a crime to steal a horse than to ruin a girl.

Louisa Lawson, Writer

Floaties

Australians never take root.

Louis Nowra, Playwright

For All Their Worth

Those who deny their distinctiveness can only pool their loneliness.

Peter Steele, Writer

For Keeps

Friend, never let anyone know what you really think of them.

Billy Hughes, Prime-Minister

For The Love Of Mike

I am an atheist. God does not need a religion.

Harry Hooton, Poet

For Whom The Road Tolls

The inability to be impressed by anything less than a fiasco of deaths is a strongly marked Australian characteristic.

Edward Kynaston, Writer

Forcing Issues
For who is there that lives and knows
the secret powers by which he grows?

Christopher Brennan, Poet

Forever Amber
Aussie blokes, opening the tinny of liquid amber, ice-cold, and particularly on a scorcher of a day, will swallow long and appreciatively, and when they come up for air, exclaim: "Je'es, *that* was good! Better than Mum's milk!"

Chris Ashton, Writer

Foul-Weather Friends
Friendship is tested in the thick years of success rather than in the thin years of struggle.

Barry Humphries, Writer-Entertainer

Freebase
The right of every person to think and determine for themselves in all matters, is at the very root of the Tree of Liberty.

Charles Harpur, Poet-Writer

Frigging In The Rigging

If a Government says "Yes", it means "Perhaps", and if it says "Perhaps", it means "No".

Randolph Bedford, Writer

Funny Farm

In Australia all people are equal with the exception of those who are not.

George Mikes, Writer

Game Of Brat And Louse

Football is a metaphor for life. Beyond question. Absolutely. It is cruel, humiliating and savage. The rules are capricious and based on the Right of Might. It is vulgar, macho, nasty and brutish.

Terry Lane, Broadcaster

Get The Feel

A lover's arms are reassuring in ways that a psychiatrist's couch cannot be, just as a neighbourly meal is more nutritious than the food it provides.

Humphrey McQueen, Historian Journalist

Get Thee To A Piggery

Local government has always been a deep, wide trough

and the hogs many, varied and insatiable.

(From "Dogfish") Susan Geason, Author

Getting A Jump On Yourself
The trouble with a good many of us is that we come to a conclusion before we arrive at the end.

F.J. "The Twinkler" Mills, Writer

Getting Folked
Advertising is the folk art of the twentieth century.

John Romeril, Playwright

Getting The Goods
Looting and pillaging are mankind's most natural form of self-expression.

Moi Moi Treborlang, Psychologist

Give It A Bash
Never pass the door of Opportunity without trying the handle.

David Low, Artist Cartoonist

Giving It Heaps
Australians endeavour to make up for quality by quantity.

Marcus Clarke, Writer

Glad Wrap
The greatest service a woman can do her community is to be happy.

Germaine Greer, Writer-Academic

Glory Be!
Seems to me that a good many men want to make angels of their wives without first taking the trouble of making saints of themselves.

Henry Lawson, Poet-Writer

Glowing Report
Like uncut opals, Australians are sometimes rough on the outside but are basically colourful and can be polished to a high brilliance.

Hayes Gordon, Actor

Go For Bust
If you can't win a debate, wreck it.

Jack Lang, Premier

Go For Your Life
You've got to be something more than nice, you've got to be adventurous.

Maria Venuti, Entertainer

Cities

If I must choose between Melbourne and Sydney I'll take Paris.

David Martin AM, Writer

Instead of despising the suburbs we should work to improve them.

Hugh Stretton, Architect

The dead heart of Australia is in the cities.

David Ireland, Writer

Nobody, it seems, likes suburbia, except the people who live there.

Craig McGregor, Writer

Show me a city's second-hand bookshops, and I will tell you what manner of citizens dwell there, and of what ancestry sprung.

Sir Walter Murdoch, Essayist

King's Cross is the nearest thing to a herd of buffalo on wheels.

George Docherty, Reverend

Go To The Rat-Pack
Why join a women's group to lobby government ministers when you can become a minister yourself?

Pauline Toner, Politician

God-awful
When man is truly humbled, when he has learnt that he is not God, then he is nearest to becoming so.

Patrick White, Novelist

Good For Nothing
Beware of people you've been kind to.

Jock Marshall, Writer

Good Grief
It's a sign of your own worth sometimes if you are hated by the right people.

Miles Franklin, Writer

Good Guts
To dream anything that you want to dream... that is the beauty of the human mind! To do anything that you want to do... that is the strength of the human will! To trust yourself to test your limits... that is the courage to succeed!

Max Walker, TV Presenter

Good Question
Don't do things for people until you know what they want.

Rose Scott, Suffragette

Got A Snout
Your nose is good enough, better probably than you deserve, be thankful that you have one of any design at all.

Tom Collins, Novelist

Govie Lovey
The proper end of government is to order things rather than people.

Brian Fitzpatrick, Historian

Grazies
You can tell the Australian hamburgers by the way the meat starts eating the lettuce.

Johnny Carson, TV Personality

Grease Fever
Just give me a meat pie and a milk shake, there's nothing like it to make a girl feel home.

Olivia Newton-John, Singer

Greenie
For Nature wild I still have zest
But human nature I love best.

Victor Daley, Poet

Ground Rules
You can't dig with the wombats and hop with the roos.

R.J. Gross, Writer

Grown-up Choir Boys
Time does not alter men — it merely unmasks them.

Hal Porter, Writer

Had The Roger
Abolition of everything is the advanced woman's raison d'etre, but there is nothing she yearns for the abolition of more than that of her natural rival — man.

The Bulletin

Hand To Mouth Combat
If the Australian language is something to be reckoned with it is because the boundary riders, larrikins, sundowners, fizgigs, diggers and other dinkum Aussies who evolved it are something to be reckoned with.

Sidney Baker, Academic-Writer

Handle With Kid Gloves
You can take the man out of the boy but you can't take the boy out of the man.

Anon

Hang On Every World
Nothing is permanent in a nation except its culture.

P.R. Stephensen, Historian

Happy Hunting Grounds
Death is about the only cheerful thing in the bush.

Henry Lawson, Poet-Writer

Hard As Nails
The more desolate and cruel is the land, the finer, in their simple way, are the people.

Francis Ratcliffe, Writer

Hard Cheese
Supermarkets stand condemned as symbols of man's inhumanity to women.

Phillip Adams, Writer-Broadcaster

Hard To Come By
I should like to be made love to by some man who didn't care in the least what I thought of him.

Rosa Praed, Writer

Hard To Swallow
It is almost impossible to assimilate an Australian into another culture.

Sir Sidney Nolan, Painter

Hat Trick
The wider the brim of the hat, the smaller the property.

Traditional Saying

Have A Goo
Everything is worth trying once — everything that is, except incest and square dancing.

Peter Ferguson, Author

Heavenly Strine
If the voice of the people is the voice of God, then all I can say is, What a shocking accent he has!

Lionel Lindsay, Writer

Hell For Whether
Nobody knows who made the Mallee, but the Devil is strongly suspected.

The Bulletin

Drinking

It's un-Australian to drive past a pub.
John Singleton, Adman-Writer

Drink is the simple word that makes life's crossword puzzle easier to elucidate.
Lennie Lower, Writer

There are very few great moments in a man's lifetime: when he's born and when he dies and when he passes his son his first beer.
Peter Kenna, Playwright

Nobody wants to die while there's rum in the bottle.
Douglas Stewart, Poet Playwright

Australians are not a nation of snobs like the English, or of extravagant boasters like the Americans, or of reckless profligates like the French; they are simply a nation of drunkards.
Marcus Clarke, Novelist

Beer makes you feel as you ought to feel without beer.
Henry Lawson, Poet-Writer

Hickey

I do hate the folk I love.

Lesbia Harford, Poet

Hit To Miss

Sometimes one feels that in Australia nothing fails like success.

Dame Leonie Kramer, Academic

Holy Dooley!

Blessed are the peacemakers — for they shall inherit a black eye.

Henry Lawson, Poet-Writer

Home Brew

No man is a hero in his own country.

Sir John Monash, Military Commander

Honesty Pays

The truth is always libellous.

George Finey, Caricaturist

Hot Under The Collar

You may keep your dignity, and I will keep my blue shirt; and we shall see which will wear the best and longest in this country.

Rev. Robert Young, Writer

Hot-Shot
Vanity can keep a man warm in winter without blankets.

Randolph Bedford, Writer

Hunters And Collectors
Australian Art must take its little gun and go out into the naughty wilderness and face the wicked big beasties like a brave little bobby.

Adrian Lawlor, Painter

I's Bigger Than Stomachs
Don't do anything you couldn't eat.

Traditional Saying

Impermanence
There's nothing so hard to find tomorrow as yesterday's paper.

Ben Chifley, Prime-Minister

Imported Vanities
It's extraordinary how every one who comes to this country of ours will persist in thinking that he has imported the first consignment of brains ever landed upon the continent.

Rolf Boldrewood, Novelist

In God We Guts
Religious emotion is secreted by the smaller intestines.

Marcus Clarke, Writer

In So Many Words
I am a fatalist and believe that what will be, will be; what is, is; and what was, was; and so on through the verbs.

Lennie Lower, Writer

In The Blood
Ethical values should appear in texts because writers and illustrators have morals, not because they want to moralise.

Paul Jennings, Writer

In The Long Run
There are no shortcuts and if there were we wouldn't take them!

Steve Moneghetti, Marathoner

In The Raw
Life is a naked goddess and we must come to her unclothed and unashamed.

Norman Lindsay, Artist-Writer

In Vein
Blood is thicker than water but then so is soup.

Lennie Lower, Writer

Inner Tube
We search everywhere for answers to our questions, to find who is responsible for our problems and then to blame and criticise, when all the time the answers lie within ourselves.

Peter Brock, Racing Car Driver

Innocents Abroad
Australians are a lot of gazelles in a dell on the edge of a jungle.

Sir Thomas Blamey, Field-Marshal

Interstate
The difference between Melbourne and Sydney is that Melbourne has Moomba and its King, while Sydney has Mardi Gras and its Queens.

Mark Knight, Cartoonist

Intimate
The word "Mateship" implies a state of things which never existed.

Henry Lawson, Poet-Writer

Inverse Reaction
If left to Australian poets, World War III would have started long ago.

Kate Jennings, Poet

Irish Breakfast
I fear death as little as to drink a cup of tea.

Ned Kelly, Bushranger

It Grows On You
Big man, big dick — small man, all dick!

Proverb

It Turns Your Stomach
The guts that got our nation going has been replaced with bellyaches.

Sir Charles Court, Premier

It's A Bit Strong
The trouble is the world expects so much of Australians. They think we all swear like troopers, drink like fish, and fight like wildcats. And that we don't know the meaning of the word "fear".

Lawson Glassop, Writer

Gambling

For Australians, gambling is a means of conversation.

Alan Ross, Writer

Everyone's entitled to life, liberty and the pursuit of horse-racing.

Banjo Paterson, Poet-Writer

Where else in the world are jockeys more revered than musicians or scientists?

Frank Hardy, Writer

The only new thing racing can do is to make the horses run backwards.

Pam Baker , Pres. VLJA

The next man that comes to you with a good tip, hit him with a club.

John Lamont, Investor

If you come out square all your life, you're in front.

Bob Cumines, Plumber

It's A Moral

Corruption happens in every country. The disquieting thing about it in Australia, as in the United States, is that people do not feel very much about it when it is happening — and forget all about it soon after.

Cyril Pearl, Writer

It's A Mug's Game

There is a widespread feeling among electors that intellect in a politician is not in harmony with the principle of representative government, hence the wily politician is prone to assume an imbecility which he does not really possess.

Sir Walter Murdoch, Essayist

It's A Snap

It is less difficult to die than watch the dying.

Patrick White, Novelist

Jiggered Traditions

I suppose there is nothing more un-Australian than a tea-bag.

Fred Daly, Politician

Jism

Seems to me the longer you read, think, talk, or write

about things that end in "ism", the less satisfactory the result.

Henry Lawson, Poet-Writer

Jungle Bruce
Yobbos are Australia's answer to the concept of the "noble savage."

Stephen Cumines, Psychologist

Jurassic Nark
In Australia alone is to be found the grotesque, the weird, the strange scribblings of nature learning how to write.

Marcus Clarke, Writer

Just So
All you've got to do is get yourself over that big hill and in at the gate.

Robin Klein, Author

Kangaroo Court
The difference between a Cabinet and a Caucus is that there are two C's in "Caucus" and only one in "Cabinet".

Anon

Keep Your Wool
Don't fly in a passion, in Aussie circles 'tis not the fashion.

William Forster, Writer

Keeping An Open Grave
The dead, I believe, are our minders.

Manning Clark, Historian

Keeping The Bastards Honest
A Member of Parliament's Bible should be the Auditor-General's Report.

Dick Butler, Politician

Kicking Butt
Nicotine should be made free so the idiot smokers can die all the quicker, and leave living to us who know how to use it.

Percy Wells Cerutty, Doctor

Kicking The Tinny
Australia is a lucky country run mainly by second-rate people who share its luck.

Donald Horne, Writer-Academic

Kid-Stakes
The average Australian boy is a cheeky brat with a leaning towards larrikinism, a craving for cigarettes, and no ambition beyond the cricket and football field.

Henry Lawson, Poet-Writer

Know The Score
You don't see any old drug addicts.

Rev. Ted Noffs, Methodist Minister

Know Who's Who
You won't understand the country without understanding something of the originals owners of it.

Xavier Herbert, Writer

Laboured Misapprehension
What sort of peculiar country is Australia where the workers' representatives predominate, and yet the capitalist system is in no danger?

Vladimir Ilich Lenin, Chief Commissar

Laid Up
It is love which makes men and women most helpless.

David Martin AM, Author

Lairs And Flares
The peculiar character of political leadership in Australia is to throw up two major personality types: the larrikin and the prima donna.

Nation Article

Lassitude
It's harder for girls.

Gavin Casey, Writer

Laughing Stock
There are only four jokes anyway: the custard pie, and the breaking of taboo, the game of words, and the thing we are each most afraid of.

Peter Goldsworthy, Writer

Laws Of The Jungle
Stuff the rule book up your arse. That's the first thing you've got to learn. Get me? Life's got its own rules.

David Williamson, Playwright

Leave For Dead
It's only when you abandon your ambitions that they become possible.

Tom Keneally, Novelist-Playwright

Love

Whoever said it was better to have loved and lost was out of their mind.

Valerie Parv, Writer

All history proves that the only vitally efficient bond between a people and their country is love.

Charles Harpur, Poet-Writer

Love is what makes the world go around — that and cliches.

Michael Symons, Writer

A lover who comes to your bed of his own accord is more likely to sleep with his arms around you all night than a lover who has nowhere else to sleep.

Germaine Greer, Writer-Academic

No one is less tolerant towards romantic longings than those who have suffered disappointment in them, who has failed to transmute them into reality.

Henry Handel Richardson, Writer

Leave It At That
Prayers grow like windless trees from silence.

Geoffrey Dutton, Writer

Leave It To Beaver
It is the essence of conservatism to leave it to others, to those who know, to decide.

Manning Clark, Historian

Left Cold
A singular disinclination to finish any work completely is a striking characteristic of Australian craftsmen.

Louisa Anne Meredith, Artist

Level-Headed
Europe has its peaks piercing the sky but we have the horizon.

Dame Mary Gilmore, Poet

Life's A Racket
Success is gauged by the amount of tension you can handle.

Moi Moi Treborlang, Psychologist

Life-Savers
A pay packet stops you from dying, it doesn't teach you how to live.

David Ireland, Novelist

Like A Charm
If you feel lost in the city, go and find yourself in the beautiful Australian bush.

Margaret Gee, Publisher

Like A Fish In Water
Surely the world we live in is but the world that lives in us.

Daisy M. Bates, Writer

Like Billyo
If the road from here to Broken Hill were paved with bibles, and that man Hitler swore an oath on every one of them, I wouldn't believe a damned word he said.

Billy Hughes, Prime-Minister

Line Of Fire
In this flaming country it's a case of far too much nature.

Glenda Adams, Writer

Live In A Box
Even St. Christopher gives the driver away over a hundred k's per hour — you've got to have God with you to survive.

Grayton Brown, Doctor

Living In Style
They build the garage into the house these days — so the six-cylinder pig can sleep with the family, like in the Middle Ages.

Barry Oakley, Writer

Loco Motive
I have always believed that if you want to do something you usually can.

A.B. Facey, Writer

Long Haul
The Wisdom and the pain will last.

Gwen Harwood, Poet

Long Live The Ashes
Who knows but that England may revive in New South Wales when it has sunk in Europe.

Joseph Banks, Botanist

Long Odds
It's not given us very often to have what we want at the height of desire.

Frank Davison, Writer

Long Stretch Of Imagination
Even a man who has been married twenty years can still be surprised at things occasionally.

Lennie Lower, Writer

Loose Eva
It's a wonder men didn't make the devil a woman.

Louisa Lawson, Writer

Lots Riding On It
An honest man, by training and racing a horse, is only helping to feed and fatten the rogues and vagabonds that live on the sport.

Steele Rudd, Writer

Lovey-Govie
For heaven's sake, why don't we try good government; it might be popular.

Ross McLean, Politician

Lowdown
In human society the warmth is mainly at the bottom.

Noel Counihan, Writer

Lucky Stroke
You don't have to be dead to be stiff

Proverb

Lure Of The Hairy Magnet
Sex has been around a long time.

Sir Eric Willis, Premier

Lurking Perks
When people say they want to maintain "the Australian way of life" it is usually pretty obvious that they mean their particular privileges.

John Anderson, Academic

Made For Each Other
For the first time in history, we have a nation for a continent, and a continent for a nation.

Edmund Barton, Prime-Minister

Marriage

Marriage is nothing more than the protest of women against the non-unionist.

Billy Hughes, Prime Minister

Matrimony: friendship under difficult circumstances.

Rose Scott, Suffragette

A man wants a wife who is more than a pillow, and yet fights everything in her that is more.

Jack Lindsay, Poet

A working man needs his beer at the end of the day before he goes home to face the tiger in the kitchen.

John Murphy, Unionist

If I ever got married again it would have to be under an anaesthetic.

Lennie Lower, Writer

A marriage is killed by words and buried by acts.

Ian Beck, Writer

Magic Tassle
Tasmania has always been and ever will be the sanatorium of tropical Australia.

Oscar De Satge, Squatter

Maintain The Wage
A man spends half his life chasing wealth, and if he catches it he spends the other half of his life trying to hold it down.

Lennie Lower, Writer

Make A Hit
If a bloke comes at you buttoning up his coat, you always king him when he's on the last button, it's just common sense.

Alan Marshall, Writer

Make Mine Last
The natural wealth belongs not only to the present, but to posterity, and all time. It is ours only in trust.

E.H. Wilson, Writer

Make Money Net
Anyone in this country who does anything for anything other than profit is either a maniac or a potential bankrupt.

James Killen, Politician

Make Or Break
The successful pioneer is the man who never spared others; the forgotten pioneer is the man who never spared himself.

Tom Collins, Novelist

Make-Belief
The ideal of the Australian is still being made.

Charles Bean, Historian

Making Mince Out Of Dons
I have nothing against Oxford men, some of our best shearers' cooks are Oxford men.

J.F. Archibald, Publisher

Masses
In Australian history, Catholics were the first ethnics.

Edmund Campion, Art-Historian

Mean Business
Even if the media were all completely honest, accurate and unbiased in all their political comments and reports, they would still uphold the interests of capitalism.

Humphrey McQueen, Historian Journalist

Meet Your Waterloo
All criticism is self-criticism.

Harry Hooton, Poet

Melbourne
A mastodon of bleeding stone.

Kenneth Slessor, Poet

Mind Over Natter
A good listener is usually thinking about something else.

Anon

Missing Godot
Everything comes too late to those who wait.

A.G. Stephens, Writer

Money For Jam
A clever writer doesn't want money, he wants marmalade.

J.F. Archibald, Publisher

Mongrel Of A Job
You always shoot your own dog.

Traditional Saying

More Than Meets The I
It's astonishing how we manage to convince ourselves of social stereotyping and how we surround ourselves with friends and props of such sameness we begin to forget there are people who live very different lives from our own.

Susan Kurosawa, Travel Writer

Mouth-Watering
You won't be famous till people start saying the worst they can of you. Don't worry! It's a good sign!

Dame Nellie Melba, Singer

Much Too Good
The world is so bad a place because there are so many good people in it.

H.E. Boote, Writer

Name The Game
A woman is a hunter without a forest.

Christina Stead, Writer

Nature's SPC
To be in harmony with life you need: Simplicity, Patience, Compassion. The proof is Nature.

Trent Nathan, Designer

Near Miss

It is always easier to be sympathetic to someone else's minority groups. They are safely out of reach and can be accorded a dignity denied our own.

Bruce Dawe, Poet

Neg Driving

What some people need is a good kick in their can't.

Wilbur Howcroft, Writer

New-Volvo Riche

One of the reasons why the working man does not resent the new upper class based on money is because he feels that he himself may enter it quite easily in his own lifetime.

John Pringle, Writer

Newcastle

Newcastle sprawls about like a drunken whore.

Peter Corris, Writer

Melbourne

Melbourne is the only place on earth where a visitor from abroad can close his eyes and wonder if there really is life before death.

Barry Humphries, Writer-Entertainer

Melbourne is a great place to be if you want to listen to your arteries hardening.

Mark Mitchell, Actor

Melbourne: Turin in the Antipodes with an Anglo-Saxon flavour.

Graham McInnes, Writer

Even Sydney stands still for three minutes and twenty odd seconds to pay homage to Melbourne, the annual armistice in the One-upmanship stakes.

Marjorie Tipping, Author

'On The Beach' is a story about the end of the world, and Melbourne sure is the right place to film it.

Neil Jillett, Journalist

Melbourne nearly always has its dress-clothes on.

Richard Twopeny, Travel Writer

Nice Drop

I don't think there's anything so profoundly depressing and so likely to encourage girls from the straight and narrow as the history of a really good woman.

Dymphna Cusack, Writer

Nimby Syndrome

I can see why a man who lives in Colorado is so anxious for all this nuclear activity to go on in Australia, an area famed among nuclear scientists for its lack of immediate proximity to their own residential area.

Fred Dagg, Media Personality

No Eluding

Christmas is always a time to be dreaded in this country.

Christina Brooks, Writer

No News Is Good News

The greatest thing that could happen in the state and the nation is when we get rid of the media. Then we would live in peace and tranquillity and no one would know anything.

Sir Joh Bjelke-Petersen, Premier

No Picnic
The problem was not created in the Garden of Eden by eating the apple, it was created on the ground by the pair.

B. Milliner, Politician

Not An Earthly
People change their dispositions as they change their climate.

Marcus Clarke, Writer

Not Within Cooee
Mates do not necessarily want to know you.

Keith Dunstan, Writer

Note From Beechworth
I count my blessings one by one. But the blessings which are not mine I seem to count more often.

David Martin AM, Author

Ockerpus
As we approach the republic, let us give consideration to adding the octopus to the national coat of arms. Wrapped around the emu and the kangaroo, it would

be a permanent celebration of three recently acquired national virtues: openmindedness, diversity and good taste.

David Dale. Writer-Journalist

Off With The Fairies
Australian history does not read like history, but like the most beautiful lies.

Mark Twain, Writer

Oh Mild West Wind
West Australians are really very proud of their somnolent climate as if they were actually responsible for it.

Robert Drewe, Author

On A Good Thing
I think men are sex objects — because they are only good for sex and not much else.

Jacki Weaver, Actor

On A Swan
In the midst of life we are in Perth.

Harry Hooton, Poet

On Our Selection
In the natural course of evolution parents must be sacrificed to their children, not children to their parents.

Louis Esson, Playwright

On The Level
In England the average man feels that he is an inferior, in America he feels that he is a superior, in Australia he feels that he is an equal.

Francis Adams, Writer

On The Make
In international affairs as in love affairs propinquity is everything.

Arthur Calwell, Opposition-Leader

On The Tear
Christ weeps over modern Sydney.

Rev. Alan Walker, Minister

On The Zeus
Alcohol is the last gift of the relenting gods.

Lennie Lower, Writer

On Tick
All I know about time is that it comes and goes too quickly.

Peter Kenna, Playwright

One Jump A Head
Wisdom is with the minority — indeed, it is generally the thought of a single mind.

Catherine Helen Spence, Novelist

One Step Ahead
Never sing in chorus; if you do you won't be heard.

J.F. Archibald, Publisher

One-Track Mind
Let the country but make the railways and the railroads will make the country.

Abraham Fitzgibbon, Designer

One-Track Mine
The only commandment that is respected in Coober Pedy is the one stating: "Don't step backwards".

Bill Peach, Writer

Men

The Australian man loves sex and hates women.
Alan Whicker, Reporter

So many Australians equate driving with masculinity: pass them and they suffer instant emasculation.

Ian Moffitt, Writer Academic

The only males allowed to show affection are footballers, poofters and reffos...
From "Shaved Fish" Susan Geason, Author

Probably the only place where a man can feel really secure from women is in a maximum security prison, except for the imminent threat of release.

Germaine Greer, Writer-Academic

The standard expression on the face of an Australian male is a frown.
Russell Braddon, Author

For the man over 40 who shouldn't smoke for health reasons, I think flirting is a suitable alternative.

A. MacKinnon, Doctor

Only Stirring
Revolution is the festival of the oppressed.

Germaine Greer, Writer-Academic

Ore Else
The best way to tell gold is to pass the nugget around a crowded bar, and ask them if it's gold. If it comes back, it's not gold.

Lennie Lower, Writer

Ouch
One has to accept pain as a condition of existence.

Morris West AM, Writer

Our Hughie
The Australian god is a two-legged brute with unnaturally developed muscles and no brains.

Henry Lawson, Poet-Writer

Out For The Count
When you hear a snake yarn, multiply the breadth by the length and divide by ten. Same calculation applies to Murray cods.

Paul Warrego, Pastoralist

Out Of Pocket
A gentleman should not talk to a lady with his hands in his pockets — unless she's his wife, in which case it's unavoidable.

Lennie Lower, Writer

Out Of The Cocoon
For most people life begins at 5 o'clock on Friday arvo.

Craig McGregor, Writer

Out Of This World
Writers re-examine and rewrite the myths of the culture in which they live.

Gabrielle Lord, Writer

Outside In
Australians invariably reserve their greatest admiration for the man from the Outback.

Charles Bean, Historian

Over The Odds
Life is littered with coincidences, of course.

Robert Dessaix, Writer-Critic

Over The Top End
In the Northern Territory it's usually a six-pack from one pub to the next.

Anon

Overload
Being human is a hideous burden.

Thea Astley, Poet

Pall-Bearing Downer
Funeral directors are not the nicest people in town, but they're the last ones to let you down.

Anon

Palmate
A true friend is one who knows you, but he likes you anyway.

Des Renford MBE, Sportsman

Paperbarks
Poets should be blue heelers not lap-dogs.

Bruce Dawe, Poet

Par For The Coarse
I don't think it pays to be honest in a dry country.

Rolf Boldrewood, Novelist

Pas de Duh
Ballet is like football. It's the most primitive form of appeal.

Sir Robert Helpmann, Dancer

Passed It
Yesterday I was rumour, today I am legend, tomorrow history.

Ian Mudie, Poet

Passing Go
Monopoly is a terrible thing, till you have it.

Rupert Murdoch, Media Magnate

Pennies For Your Thought
The only people really keeping the spirit of irony alive in Australia are taxi-drivers and homosexuals.

Barry Humphries, Writer-Entertainer

Perth
A city in transition, not sure where it is going but obviously going there fast.

Craig McGregor, Writer

Petty Point

All small chiefs are bastards.

Sorin Dascalu, Architect

Picking Losers

Our first settlers were chosen by England's best judges.

Sir Douglas Copland, Economist

Piece Of Cake

The great secret of being useful and successful is to admit of no difficulties.

Sir George Gipps, Governor

Playing With Matches

Anyone who doesn't watch rugby league is not a real person. He's a cow's hoof, an ethnic, senile or comes from Melbourne.

John Singleton, Adman-Writer

Pleasant Stock

It is hard to quarrel with men who only wish to be innocently happy.

James "Down Under" Froude, Writer

Money

Money, like matter, is indestructible.

G.F. Amsberg, Judge

England's the best country in the world when a man has made his money, but there's no place like Australia for making it.

Rolf Boldrewood, Writer

I saw bank booms, land booms, silver booms, Northern Territory booms, and they all had one thing in common — they always burst.

Banjo Paterson, Poet-Writer

Enthusiasm is a poor vote catcher, and mere patriotism is valueless, but a strong bank account can win seats every time.

George Meudell, Writer

Big Money is always on the Lord's side.

Randolph Bedford, Politician

A man of business is one who becomes possessed of other people's money without bringing himself under the power of the law.

Marcus Clarke, Novelist

Plonk vs Shonk
Without doubt it is easier to recognise costly vintages than to live contentedly on the smell of an oily rag.

Tom Collins, Novelist

Plugged Up
Time, the flood that does not flow.

Kenneth Slessor, Poet

Pom de Terre
Everything in Tasmania is more English than is England herself.

Anthony Trollope, Writer

Poor Excuse
Charity is a hateful thing because it is created by poverty.

Frank Hardy, Writer

Pop You Later
Populate, or perish!

Billy Hughes, Prime-Minister

Power Points
The essence of democracy is respect for minorities, not rule by majorities.

Sir John Latham, Chief-Justice

Pray Safe
The church has given the impression of protecting the protected and neglecting the neglected.

Rev. Ted Noffs, Methodist Minister

Pray With Fire
Why, strike me pink, I'd sooner drink
With a bloke sent up for arson
Than a rain-beseeching, preaching, teaching,
Blanky, cranky parson.

Traditional Bush Song

Product Recall
Wake up, look around, memorise what you see, it may be gone tomorrow.

Michael Dransfield, Poet

Punch Line
It's fine for any kid to have a good left hand. But being able to use the right nouns and verbs lasts longer, and it pays off better in most cases.

Lionel Rose, Boxer

Punt Of A Thing
Love is a gamble, an' there ain't no certs.

C.J. Dennis, Poet

Punting The Styx
There was a strange deep satisfaction in watching a funeral; it made them feel almost smug that they were still alive, while they still stood, not only alive and kicking, but with a good chance of winning the double on Saturday.

Ruth Park, Writer

Push In Tab
So long as Australians have beer and betting they are all right.

Miles Franklin, Writer

Putting The Acid On God
Men think they are pious when they are only bilious.

Marcus Clarke, Writer

Queensland
The trouble is that Queensland gets branded as being part of Australia.

Sir Joh Bjelke-Petersen, Premier

Quiet The Worms
Don't worry about the stars, go for the oysters

George Gibson, Poet

Rain, Hail But Shine

Melbourne's population is not given to hide its light under a bushel.

Anthony Trollope, Writer

Ready Worship

I do not think it unfair to say that the worst Australian characteristic is a reverence for money, and for the artificial social distinctions created by its possession in any quantity.

Martin Boyd, Writer

Real Life

Anyone who thinks all mankind's divided into good, bad, and middlin' — don't know much.

Rolf Boldrewood, Novelist

Red Alert

No poet had ever written a sonnet to fried tomatoes. And yet they are supposed to be able to discern beauty and capture visions.

Lennie Lower, Writer

Poems

Never admit the pain,
Bury it deep;
Only the weak complain,
Complaints is cheap.
Dame Mary Gilmore, Poet

While you live, live in clover,
For when you're dead,
You're dead all over.
Squizzy Taylor, Criminal

In the land where sport is sacred,
where the laborer is a god,
You must pander to the people,
make a hero of a clod!
Henry Lawson, Poet-Writer

Look for your profits in the hearts of friends
For hating never paid no dividends.
C.J. Dennis, Poet

Australian-born,
Australian bred
Long in the leg, and short in the head.
Traditional

Poems

Not the Rhine, the Niger or the Thames,
sluggish with history and reflected flames,
Is worth a drop of Yarra.
John Streeter Manifold, Poet

Peace is a country to be won
by you and me, and everyone.
Jack Lindsay, Poet

Let the word: Australian!
Dignify the lowliest man.
Arthur Baylebridge, Poet

Joy is bloody fleetin'
Life is bloody short
Wot's the use of wastin' it
All on bloody sport?
C.J. Dennis, Poet

From 10 to 1
There's nothing done
From 2 to 3
We begin to see
That from 3 to 4
There'll be nothing more!
Edmund Barton, Prime Minister

Rev Head
Live dangerously, live dangerously, there aren't
enough people in the world who live dangerously.

Billy Hughes, Prime Minister

Revise The Refugee
Men do not emigrate in despair, but in hope.

Sir William Hancock, Historian

Revolting History
Australia progressed by a series of little rebellions.

Leslie Clement Haylen, Politician

Rings True
I love youse all.

Jeff Fenech, Champion Boxer

Robber Barons
This country is only fit for thieves and rich men.

Lachlan Macquarie, Governor

Rolling Against Gravity
It's a long way to the top if you want to rock 'n' roll.

Bon Scott, Songwriter

Rooted
People who sit tight usually remain where they are.

F.J. "The Twinkler" Mills, Writer

Roots
What is Nationalism but the football-team spirit?

Xavier Herbert, Writer

Rose Among Thorns
Women have very little idea of how much men hate them.

Germaine Greer, Writer-Academic

Rough Stuff
Australians have a notion that crudity is a sign of vigour and illiteracy of bold originality.

Louis Esson, Playwright

Rough Trades
Drink is stronger than unionism.

Henry Lawson, Poet-Writer

Rugger Pukkah
The difference between Soccer and Rugby is that Soccer is a thugs' game played by gentlemen while Rugby is a gentlemen's game played by thugs.

John Gurney, Writer

Rule Of Thumb
A community that endures a contemptible law is itself contemptible.

A.G. Stephens, Writer

Run Down Country
It has long been accepted that one of our most pronounced national traits is that of self-denigration, of which the reverse side is the right to denigrate others, referred to as knocking.

Charmian Clift, Writer

Running On Retreads
Some men don't find women attractive unless they're ugly.

Ian Stocks, Academic-Filmmaker

S.O.L.
If you value your liver you'll eat plain omelets and drink only wine and beer.

Graham Kerr, Cook

Save The Day
Life is a diminishing asset and like any asset it should not be wasted.

John Capsanis, Legal Practitioner

Schizophrenic Academic
Australian intellectuals want their country to be "different" and Australian but dislike nearly everything which makes it different and which other people recognize as Australian.

John Douglas Pringle, Writer

See The Writing On The Wall
As soon as the scrub is cleared, the houses built, the natives dispossessed, a new country must set about furnishing itself with a literature.

Peter Conrad, Writer

Self-Reflection
The rich always have lots of mirrors in their houses because they like what they see in them.

Peter Corris, Author

Sell A Dummy
Advertising is simply, and only, the poor man's substitute for door to door selling.

John Singleton, Adman-Writer

Serves Them Right
Unionism came to the Australian bushman as a religion.

W.G. Spence, Writer

Shaping Up A Beaut

Nobody wants a girl whose beauty is imperceptible to all but him.

Germaine Greer, Writer-Academic

Shattered Dreams

"I was only joking" — are the four saddest words in the world.

Jessica Anderson, Writer

"Shaved Fish"

The space between divorcing couples is like the Somme, littered with the bodies of the innocent and the foolhardy.

Susan Geason, Author

Shine And Punishment

Good women when they die, are born again as men.

Victor Daley, Poet

Spread

When happiness comes, it's so thick and smooth and uneventful, it's like nothing at all.

Helen Garner, Author

Poems

The wise old owl sat on the oak
The more he heard, the less he spoke
The less he spoke, the more he heard.
We should be always like that wise old bird.
J. Bart Cummings AM, Horse Trainer

Our town's a pub and general store
What's the use of any more?
Slim Dusty, Singer

Many fools make money
According to the rules.
But what is yet more funny,
Money makes many fools.
Bartlett Adamson, Writer

If you've a case without a Judge,
It's clear your case will never budge;
But if a Judge you have to face
The chances are you'll lose your case.
Norman Lindsay, Artist-Writer

Shining Spirit
If you want real practical wisdom go to an old washerwoman patching clothes at the Rocks with a black eye, and you'll hear more true philosophy than a Parliament of men will talk in a twelve-month.

Louisa Lawson, Writer

Shoosh Vs Moosh
Better silence than falsehood.

Tom Collins, Novelist

Shore Tempered
Australians always seem a bit on the edge.

Rudyard Kipling, Writer

Shrinking Heaven
Psychology is the theology of the 20th century.

Harry Hooton, Poet

Sixth Sense
We occupy, all of us, our own five-walled tower of senses. The throne in the central chamber is the throne of intuition, so often the snoozing one.

Hal Porter, Writer

Sin Bin
I'd rather be a lover than a saint.

Lesbia Harford, Poet

Sitcom
The malaise of the Australian people is reflected in our Parliament.

Edward St John, Legal Practitioner

Skipping The Skipper
Just because someone is no longer the captain of a side, it doesn't mean he's not still the best batsman in the team.

John Capsanis, Legal Practitioner

Sleeping Bewdy
Sydney is a place that will some day wake terribly from its magic sleep.

D.H. Lawrence, Novelist

Slicing The Cold Turkey
Come down slowly, the world is hard to land on.

Michael Dransfield, Poet

Slide Of Cake

The Lamington is a delicious sponge square dipped in melted chocolate and desiccated coconut which progresses through the digestive tract with all the ease of a building block.

The Bulletin

Slight Collar Worker

A kind man has more importance in the eye of God than a man with a holy book.

Peter Carey, Novelist

Slim Chance

This is the age of Diet-Lard.

Mark Knight, Cartoonist

Slow-Poke

The man who hasn't a male mate is a lonely man indeed, or a strange man, though he have a wife and family.

Henry Lawson, Poet-Writer

Small Poppies

Anzac Day is a celebration of the essential ordinariness and the common human-ness of man.

Donald Horne, Writer-Academic

Politicians

There's no point in being subtle in Australia.
Paul Keating, Prime Minister

All the open spaces in this country aren't in the Outback, a lot of them are between the ears of ministers in the Government.
Bill Hayden, Governor-General

Too many cooks and not enough Indians spoil the golden egg.
Sir Joh Bjelke-Petersen, Premier

Freedom from fear can never be separated from freedom from want.
Herbert Evatt, Opposition Leader

Politicians are like bananas: They come in green, turn yellow and there's not a straight one in the bunch.
John Norton, Politician

The only type of man who can be happy in the job of Treasurer is one who by nature is a sadist and has a heart of stone.
Harold Holt, Prime Minister

Small Wonder
Tasmania teaches you how briefly human history has interrupted the time of earth, and reveals how frail are all our efforts to make ourselves at home.

Peter Conrad, Writer

Smart Cockies
All men are lawyers in the bush.

Henry Lawson, Poet-Writer

Smarties
People wrapped up in themselves make a mighty small package.

Caroline Chisholm, Early Social Worker

Smash Hit
It is my opinion that if there is no fight at a party, the party isn't a success.

Lennie Lower, Writer

Smell Burnin'
Melbourne is like a distant war in which I lost my life.

Bruce Dawe, Poet

Sneaky Clean
I have generally found it that people consider that

government and the public may be duped and plundered without crime as long as it is done neatly.

Francis Greenway, Architect

Soaks
Australians "learn" their culture.

Donald Horne, Writer-Academic

Sold Out
Mistrust popularity, the rock on which many a good man has wrecked his soul.

Sir Walter Murdoch, Essayist

Sore Spot
To be accurate is not to be right.

Shirley Hazzard, Writer

Sounding Off
Just because you smoke dope and listen to rock and roll, don't think you're somehow magically morally okay.

Peter Carey, Novelist

Stack On An Act
Be not led into the wretchedness of right conduct.

David Ireland, Novelist

Stairway To Heaven
Australians like to think that the average is divine.

Sir William Keith Hancock, Historian

Stalemate
From the moment that one lands in Australia, stagnation begins.

Hardy Wilson, Traveller

Stand Alone
To be fair to Australians, they don't afford excessive respect to anybody. It's one of their virtues.

Malcolm Muggeridge, Writer

Standing Ground
We believe it is the loneliness and harsh seasons, the glare and the flies, the distance from help and the rest of the world, that makes a man.

Murray Bail, Writer

Starry Eyed
Hunters and lovers see best in the dark.

Geoffrey Dutton, Writer

Politics

No country deserves politicians as bad as these.

John Douglas Pringle, Writer

Advertising men and politicians are dangerous
if they are separated. Together they are
diabolical.

Phillip Adams, Writer-Broadcaster

The system of government we have in Australia
is socialism for the rich and free enterprise for
the poor.

Bob Ellis, Filmmaker-Writer

Make no mistakes about referendums. Their
results are notorious. You couldn't introduce
free beer by referendums.

John Walsh, Writer

I have often thought it must require a high
degree of intelligence to look as unintelligent as
some of our politicians contrive to look.

Sir Walter Murdoch, Essayist

The Labor Party preaches socialism and the
Liberal Party practices it.

Lang Hancock, Tycoon

Starve The Bardies!
Why be difficult when with a little extra effort you can make yourself impossible?

Percy Grainger, Composer

Staying A Head
Once you have become a drug addict, you will never want to be anything else.

Michael Dransfield, Poet

Step In The Right Direction
There are many ways to walk gently in the world.

Anne Deveson, Writer-Broadcaster

Stick-In-The-Mud
The best way to create a radical is to hit a conservative person over the head with a police truncheon.

Keith Suter, Doctor

Stiff Cheddar
Rookwood Cemetery is full of indispensable men.

Ben Chifley, Prime Minister

Stiff Luck
Australia is a beautiful country to die in.

Will Dyson, Cartoonist

Stiff Sentence
Love is hard; if we were condemned to it we would complain.

Christina Stead, Writer

Stirring The Possum
The joy of cooking in Australia is that you can break the rules.

Serge Densereau, Chef

Strap-Hangers
The abject popular tendency to deify and worship the mere show of greatness lies at the very root of the tattered poor's misery.

Charles Harpur, Poet

Strictly For The Birds
You don't have to be solemn to be serious.

Oskar Spate, Writer

Strike A Light
We just have to stumble on blindly with God's mercy raining down on us like thunderbolts.

Peter Kenna, Playwright

Stuffed
Rather than commit suicide, Australians are more apt to commit smugness.

Elspeth Huxley, Writer

Sunny Side Up
I feel beautiful because I'm learning.

Ruby Eleanor Brown, Five-year old

Surrender The Think
The worst aspect of war is not the danger of wounds and death from the enemy, but the submission of one's body and soul to brutes and fools in authority.

Martin Boyd, Writer

Symptom's Desert
Being Australian is a kind of painless disease — it doesn't start hurting until you leave the place.

Barry Oakley, Writer

Take For Grunted
One man is just as good as another, in fact better.

Harry Hooton, Poet

Take The Mickey And Run
It's not until you're actually past forty that you realise that the expression "Life begins at forty" was meant in an ironic sense.

Bill Garner, Writer

Sex

History shows that you can make prostitution illegal, but you can't make it unpopular.

Jim McClelland, Politician

Men see coitus as the meat in the sandwich of foreplay and afterplay; women see it as the icecream in a Bombe Alaska of intimate emotional exchange.

Beatrice Faust, Author

Women put up with sex to get marriage and men put up with marriage to get sex.

Anonymous

A wowser is a gentleman who uses a contraceptive as a book-mark for his Bible.

Jock Marshall, Writer

Country tarts would root a wombat if they thought he was going to be a doctor one day.

David Williamson, Playwright

Fucking made all of us.

Sebastian Hogbotel, Writer

Taking To The Hills
It has been said that people cannot feel really at home in any environment until they have transformed the natural shapes around them by infusing them with myth.

Vance Palmer, Writer

Tale Spin
A story is never an accurate translation of life, it is always larger than life, so never spoil a good one for the sake of the truth.

Alan Marshall, Writer

Talk And Sleaze
Australian politics is the monopoly of men whose verbose incompetence is only equalled by their jovial corruption.

Francis Adams, Writer

Tarred With The Same Brush
It was in Australia that I gained my first impressions of the beauty of the world, and it was the Bush that taught me.

Tom Roberts, Artist

Tasmania
Tasmania is a very big little island.

M. Barnard Eldershaw, Writer-Historian

Taut A Lesson
Politics is both a fine art and an inexact science.

Sir Robert Menzies, Prime-Minister

Teachings Of The Moolah
The best way to help the poor is not to become one of them.

Lang Hancock, Tycoon

Teflon Brains
Some minds are not only open for the truth to enter but also to pass on through by way of a ready exit without pausing anywhere along the route.

Sister Elizabeth Kenny, Nurse

Temple Of Dom
Appearances to the contrary, Australia has an ingrained spirituality, courtesy of Koori-dom. The land pulses with ghosts and the spirits of place. Like it or not, fight it or not, each of us is aware — inside, and no so far down — that the whole joint is a church and we are all priests.

Steve J. Spears, Playwright

Test Players
Most bastards aren't real bastards, they are only trying out.

Denis Kevans, Poet

That'll Be The Day
I dare say the day will come when we shall all have to go to a higher court than this. Then we will see who is right and who wrong.

Ned Kelly, Bushranger

The Almighty Well-Being
The religion of Australia is its standard of living.

Lloyd Ross, Economist

The Average Aussie
He can't ride a horse. He has never shorn a sheep. He wouldn't know how to cook a damper if he were starving to death. He'd fail to recognise a billabong if one darted out of the long grass and bit him on the ankle.

Ken Collie, Writer

The Big Doop
For all its vastness and aloof indifference, Australia is a fragile land that is very vulnerable.

Phillip Drew, Author

Sports

There is nothing so momentary as a sporting achievement and nothing so lasting as the memory of it.

Greg Dening, Writer

There's two things you can be certain of: dying, and getting the arse as a football coach.

Royce Hart, Football Coach

Waiting for Cronulla to win a grand final is like leaving the porch light on for Harold Holt.

Jack Gibson, Coach

Crudity is an Australian specialty. We're trying to get it put in the Olympics.

Barry Oakley, Writer

Sport should be for everyone and anyone, it should be good for us and, above all, it should be healthy.

Sue Williams, Author-Journalist

Sport to many Australians is life and the rest a shadow.

Donald Horne, Academic-Writer

The Big Squeeze
Why should Australia's role be the constant sponge lying in the Pacific?

Robin Boyd, Writer

The Chronic In Continent
The Australians were wise to choose such a large country, for of all the people in the world they clearly require the most space.

Kenneth Galbraith, Writer

The Great Australian Bite
The Australian cadger has developed the technique of the bite until it is almost one of the arts.

Dymphna Cusack Writer

The Greedhouse Effect
Green instead of greed.

Dr Bob Brown, Environmentalist

The House Union Jack Built
The English gave Australia its laws, the Scots its money and the Irish its humour.

Edmund Campion, Art-Historian

The J(unk) Curve
The ultimate product of economic life is garbage.

Sir Garfield Barwick, Attorney-General

The Living End
Drink, dirt, and sloth will produce the same effects all over the world.

Henry Kingsley, Writer

The Longest Weekend
If the Apocalypse came Australians would probably think it was a public holiday.

Louis Nowra, Playwright

The Old Mysterious Trinity
Australia is a three party country with a one party press.

Macmahon Ball, Academic

The Other Shaky Isle
There are not many countries in the world where people get the DT's on beer. Australia is one of them.

E. Cunningham-Dax, Doctor

The Plucky Country
The world is as full today as ever it was of the shining

virtues of courage in danger and fortitude in adversity. They are to be found in all sort of odd places; in the lonely bush and in the crowded slum; the heroic is everywhere at home.

Sir Walter Murdoch, Essayist

The Push

The aggressive insistence on the worth and unique importance of the common people seems to me to be one of the fundamental Australian characteristics.

Hartley Grattan, Historian

The Rest Is Silence

It is my belief that if more people lay down and rested in their spare time, there would be fewer arrests, divorces, bankruptcies, suicides and marriages.

Lennie Lower, Writer

The Strong Of It

Labour is the poor man's property.

George Loveless, Writer

The Wank Tank

There are four broad styles of Australian car design: Domestic, Functional, Speed and Lair.

The Bulletin

Success

If life hands you a lemon, make lemonade!

Kamahl AO, Singer

There is no success without trying.

Matthew Sandblom, Publisher

First it's one thing and then it's another, something leads up to something else and this and that, and before you know where you are - there you are!

Lennie Lower, Writer

You can argue with a dead man but you can't win.

Stephen Cumines, Psychologist

If you have to sin, sin bravely.

Sir Roderick Carnegie, Businessman

Pioneering takes sweat and discouragement, hardship and long waiting for success, a lifetime of battling.

Dora Birtles, Novelist

The White As A Ghost
The problems of the Australian aborigine will only be solved when the white man no longer causes fear in the black man.

Egon Erwin Kisch, Travel Writer

The Yucky Country
Never was a continent so naturally clean and made so dirty as Australia.

Randolph Bedford, Writer

Think Nothing Of It
Anyone who stares long enough into the distance is bound to be mistaken for a philosopher or mystic in the end.

Patrick White, Novelist

Think Tank
The human being is not a spirit within a body, or a body enclosing a spirit, but a complete and miraculous entity whose ultimate genius is its awareness of itself.

Eleanor Dark, Writer

Three-Ring Circus
The three never-failing accompaniments of advancing civilisation are a racecourse, a public house and a gaol.

Rev. John Dunmore Lang, Writer

Time Lags
The past has bequeathed to Australians a long list of unmentionable words.

Manning Clark, Historian

Tits On A Bull
Men are the uselessest, good-for-nothingest, clumsiest animal in the world.

Miles Franklin, Writer

To A Void
Nature's all right but it's too big for most people.

Patrick White, Novelist

Too Clever
Australia is a country high on ego and low on self-esteem.

Kate Jennings, Poet

Too Far Gone
A country of great distances tends to breed narrow minds.

Thomas Wood, Writer

Too Much Of A Good Thing
It's the best country to get out of that I was ever in.

Henry Lawson, Poet-Writer

Too Much Of A Muchness
Where all are assumed to be equal there can be no true leadership.

William Baylebridge, Poet

Touchy Subject
To make friends with an Australian is like making friends with a very nervous ill-treated animal.

Reginald Thompson, Writer

Toughening The Malleable
Three raw eggs for breakfast, then a quick jog around the park with a coupla jerseys on, and by the time the footy season gets under way you'll be as fit as a mallee bull.

Desmond O'Grady, Writer

Sydney

Sydney — a city of three hundred thousand souls expanded into three million people. Melbourne is the same but not quite so active.

J.R. Gross, Writer

Sydney is the only town in Australia where crime is a major spectator sport.

Bob Ellis, Writer\Film-maker

Sydney: New York without intellect.

David Williamson, Playwright

There were no real seasons in Sydney, only festivals.

Margaret McClusky, Writer

Sydney? That's a strange name for a city. Why didn't they call it Fred?

Robert Morley, Actor

No great city in the history of the world was born under so cruel a star.

John Douglas Pringle, Writer

Two-Piece Suit
Every country develops its own indigenous quality when people and countries become one.

Pino Bosi, Writer

Two-Timers And Part-Timers
Mankind may be broadly divided into two classes — perpetual liars, and intermittent liars.

Tom Collins, Novelist

Under The Right Wing
This stuff about the meek inheriting the earth is a lot of bullshit. The weak need the strong to look after them.

Bob Hawke, Prime-Minister

Under Wraps
So much of Australia's history took place outside the law where there was more attempt to hide it than record it.

Eric Charles Rolls, Writer

Unfinished Business
We have the only country in the world that is still to make.

Charles Bean, Historian

Television

Television interviewing is like a jukebox. You put in your 20-cent question, you get your one-minute answer.

Andrew Denton, Media Personality

You are what you watch.

Mark Knight, Cartoonist

Adam's first law of television: the weight of the backside is greater than the force of the intellect.

Phillip Adams, Writer-Broadcaster

No more message-stick;
Lubras and lads
Got television now
Mostly ads.

Oodgeroo Noonuccal, Poet

Repeat programmes are only repeat programmes for those who have already seen them.

Len Mauger, Managing Director

Union Jack Off

The Australian ego is a crude and bastardly conglomeration of the basest contents of English Nonconformism, Scottish Presbyterianism and Irish Catholicism.

Norman Lindsay, Artist-Writer

Unions

An army of lions led by asses.

Henry Hyde Champion, Politician

Unspeakable Hunger

Australians swallow more syllables than any other single item of consumption.

Sir Hermann Black, Academic

Up The Creek Without A Camus

I have always thought that the lightning rod of a national literature is located somewhere amongst the outsiders of a society, the minorities, the dispossessed and the oppressed. As Graham Greene said, "genuine culture is always in opposition."

Rosie Scott, Author

Up The Spout

Nature here is nearly worn out.

Robert Ross, Lt-Governor

Up To Know Good
One difference between men and women is that, at any rate, a woman knows when she is bad.

Rosie Scott, Suffragette

Villa Casa Porch
The veranda is that frail lightweight addition which people fleeing from the European house can escape to.

Phillip Drew, Author

Wakey-Wakey
I am convinced that a man, until he sees bullets flying around him, does not basically realise that war is serious, that the enemy is out to kill him.

David Campbell, Poet

Water On The Brain
Don't pray for rain — dam it.

James Moorhouse, Bishop

We Are The Past
The dead are not merely the dead. They are our fathers, mothers, grandfathers, grandmothers. We are their heredity.

Brian Elliott, Teacher

Women

When women are free, we'll see other emotions, no love. Love is a slave emotion, like a dog's.

Christina Stead, Novelist

Women look a lifetime ahead.

Ernestine Hill, Writer

The Australian character comes from the masculine principle in its women, the feminine in its men.

Patrick White, Novelist

Women have it easy. They can fail all their lives and nobody holds it against them.

Alma De Groen, Playwright

Girls! girls! Those of you who have hearts, and therefore a wish for happiness and husbands, never develop a reputation of being clever. It'll put you out of the matrimonial running as effectually as though it had been circulated that you had leprosy.

Miles Franklin, Writer

Women

Woman's enfranchisement means man's enslavement.

J.F. Archibald, Publisher

Convent girls never leave the church, they just become feminists.

Blanche D'Alpuget, Author

You are only liberated when you realise just how awful you are.

Germaine Greer, Writer-Academic

It is a hard life being a eucalypt, nearly as hard as being a woman, a matter of holding on grimly, and good judgment.

Kylie Tennant, Writer

Feminism is not feminine, it merely dresses woman in man's trousers and tags her with a list of male attributes.

Dulcie "Queen of Bohemia" Deamer, Author

Show me a woman in power, and I will show you a despot.

Barbara Baynton, Writer

Wearing Thin
Losing weight is not difficult. That's why so many of us have done it so often.

Valerie Parv, Writer

Westies
Western Australia is the best country in the world to run through an hour-glass.

Anthony Trollope, Writer

What Are Ya?
Australia has been unspeakably retarded by an unfortunate dispute among geographers as to whether it is a continent or an island.

Ambrose Bierce, Humourist

What It Takes
It is not hard work, either mental or physical, that kills a man; it is anxiety and worry.

James Scullin, Prime Minister

When The Fat Lady Slangs
The reason Australians make such good opera singers is you don't speak a good English.

Carlo Felice Cillario, Conductor

Whichever Way The Wind Blows
We get not only the politicians we deserve, but the weather as well.

Howell Witt, Bishop

White Injustice
In the minds of all blacks, the Australian claim to nationhood continues to rest on injustice and hypocrisy.

Kevin John Gilbert, Writer

Whoppers
The tender Australian public only tolerates flattery and that in its cheapest form.

Charles Bean, Historian

Winning Hands Up
It is better to be defeated on principle than to win on lies.

Arthur Calwell, Opposition-Leader

Wouldn't Read About It
There is no such thing as a true history.

Kate Grenville, Novelist

Write-offs
You never find authors in Australia starving in a garret — they couldn't afford one.

Paul Buddee, Writer

X Rated

There's no-one so ex as an ex.

Sir Robert Menzies, Prime Minister

Year Zero

Nothing substantial is ever built up when each generation feels it is starting from scratch.

C.B. Christesen, Academic

Yellow Sages

Resignation is selfishness under another name, it is cowardice under a white veil of goodness.

Louisa Lawson, Writer

Yowie Country

There's an absolute ultimate truth about Australia, all wrapped up in stringybark and guarded over by bunyips.

Colin MacInnes, Author

You've Gotta Win It To Be In It

The history of mankind is written by the victors.

Manning Clark, Historian